While every precaution has been taken in the preparation of this book, the publisher assumes no responsibility for errors or omissions, or for damages resulting from the use of the information contained herein.

CONFIDENTIAL: DIARY OF A MAN

First edition. March 25, 2023.

Copyright © 2023 J.R. Hall.

ISBN: 979-8223643883

Written by J.R. Hall.

Table of Contents

Confidential: Diary Of A Man 1
PREFACE 5
Epilogue 83

Confidential:
Diary Of
A Man
J. R. Hall

Copyright © 2023 Johnny Hall
All rights reserved.

DEDICATION

I want to dedicate this book to my children Maximillian, Maverix, & Mars for you are the 3 gifts that have shown me my own manhood. Although I may have started writing these thoughts long before I held you all — know each of you is the push & passion with which it came to life. I also want to thank their mother Kierra, you have walked with me into adulthood, and becoming a man and you a woman —has been such an eye-opening journey. Thank You to my family for always believing in me and never shying away from giving me love in every moment. To Rachael, my mother who did everything in her power to expose me to the vastness of possibility and not the funnel of limitations, Thank You. My brother Jordyn, who has shown me that laughter and serious focus can both share space together. My grandmother Deborah, that being kind never goes unnoticed. To my late Grandfather Johnny Sr., who demanded respect and instilled that into me, Thank You! My maternal grandparents showed me LOVE can last as long as you let it and nature teaches you life better than any movie or daytime soap opera, even though you have not missed one in decades [Rosie]. Also, to Charles, my grandfather, thank you for bestowing wisdom on me before my heart and mind could catch up to what you spoke into my spirit and soul. Lastly, Ms. Rose [my second-grade teacher] if you ever get an opportunity to read this, I want to send my deepest thank you. Your words and care as I was in the 2nd grade showed me so much, you taught me to bet and work on myself and never settle. I grew up with that and I am sure you are blessed and happy somewhere but your words made this little boy want to grow into a never-content but always grateful man, so my writing flourished along with so many other things.

Table of Contents
DIARY OF A MAN

DEDICATION

PREFACE

THE FOUNDATION
GROUNDBREAKING
LOCATION
DESIGNS
CONSTRUCTION
DEVELOPMENT
INNOVATION
RESISTANCE
ELEVATION

Epilogue
ABOUT THE AUTHOR

PREFACE

Journal Entry – July 10th, 2016

    I in darkness have found peace, that peace is closure and letting go for holding on grabs you towards directions not meant for you. The world lacks love and discipline. It lacks passion and understanding. As we all have prejudice and selfish ways, we see only how it affects our own psyche and our own personal palette of colors. We dare not explore, for most are more frightened of growth than they are of destruction. For they revel in death, toying with the inevitable and almost looking to induce the process faster than one can imagine. Focus is lost, and falls victim to a lack thereof. The facade of my freedom is an ignorant expression of indecision. I in my 25 years have learned a great deal and continue to seek more about the repercussions of risk. Understanding it is far more beneficial than those quaint aspirations. In my times of famine, I have found renewed hunger. In my times of drought found suitable thirst, a storm whispered you are weak and not strong enough to weather this. In a cynical grin, I replied, " I am The Fucking Storm." I have loved, I have given, I have laughed, I have cried, I have gained, I have lost. Yet the most satisfying feeling was understanding how the dark was the essence of light. Darkness was all grasping all seeking. In my life, I knew my presence was divine for that I had to learn that praise and respect come in many forms.

    I write to cleanse -I read to refresh- I love to heal- I fight to my death

    "So, worry not who speaks ill of you in private. Worry not about who laughs at your failures. Worry not about who leaves as you explore. Worry not about who does not want to conquer with you, simply worry about those who will be able to benefit from the gifts you bestow on this world. Even if those people who you stopped worrying about initially are those most touched by it."

-Johnny R. Hall III

Life is precious, it materializes and falls apart swiftly. This memoir of my personal journal is to highlight not merely my flaws but my strengths. To all men understand that you have a significant and purposeful reason to be here, to boys who are growing into men realize it takes time to build greatness. Once you see the abundance in yourself that is how others are allowed to access you, FLOURISH & PROSPER ALWAYS!

THE FOUNDATION

A product of my environment, yet an explorer of the universe.

Today was my grandfather's burial service and oddly death has become normal to me. I've been to far more funerals than weddings. I've seen far more violence than loving bliss.

I see my siblings and family are all cut from the same product. Some would say it's not really good, others find it to be the only peace they know.

My grandfather luckily wasn't at the funeral due to violence. The streets didn't consume him; he lived a life of playfulness. He left behind a woman of love and compassion. He touched lives.

Even though he himself was a product of his environment.

I admire my grandfather for beating his statistical odds but better yet for being a necessary person to my success.

I'm not perfect nor will I claim to be but my grandfather made me a CHAMPION. A winner and most importantly a diligent & selfless person.

I'm many things but because of him, I know that and live it. As we lay his body to rest. I know that his WILL and GRACE live through me.

Today was perfect and it was a testament to his life success and it never equates to anything but his character!

If I can be a fraction of that impactful, then I know his soul will rest well.

Love Always,
Your Sunday Baby!
Dear Diary,

Today I woke up frustrated, thankful but frustrated. I feel stagnant turning my wheels in a wayward and unnatural way. Pessimism is slowly attempting to put out my flame. Today is short and quiet. I am alone navigating my emotions —no I am not miserable so I require no party or entourage to partake with me. Over the horizon the sun is setting, what if today is my last day. I feel unfulfilled, truthfully what have I accomplished to give to the world. Have I let my children down? My son respects me but who am I? The question my soul asks me?

    Today felt powerless, the reins slowly stripped from the grasp of my hands, it was out of control. God, I gave a call but today it just rang. I am positive he is busy with something and someone far more important as my issue is one of the self-inflicted and self-discovering proportions. Today was a day but it blurred quickly tonight. The sun shined but I dare not feel it atop my skin.

    Am I being punished, am I being pushed, am I simply being held in place? Somehow today I broke down and not into tears because well for some reason or another it is hard for me to cry. It has been almost two years since I have cried. That is when my Granny passed, I was demolished. Does my fleeting self-assurance come off as arrogant because underneath all this flesh and perception of strength? Is a fragile man who feels abandoned. Discussing my feelings, yeah not something men do, is what I was told and I did not see my mother do it either– so I for damn sure have to be tough for her. My daughter & son cannot respect a man who embodies weakness so I for damn sure have to be a protector for them. They already do not want to see black men be strong, they already fight to weaken a black man's strength, and they already fight for a black man to lose his place.

    So, I ask myself, Who is They???

    TODAY was null and lost.

    Today I ask, "Who Am I?"

    Today was:

    soft Jazz and smelled of heavy scotch...

    A man's foundation is such a quintessential piece of his existence, a goal is to define it from the core. Intangible features not aesthetics—character traits that build upon your legacy—discipline, courage, integrity, intelligence, strength, wisdom, charisma. When you have an upbringing that borders on strong values, your ability to grow and build upon is a transition of imagination paired with persistence and diligent hard work.

Yet what happens when your foundation is laid upon the wrong elements. Not sturdy, just laid aimlessly in a faux attempt to say that it was done, the illusion of quality merely masked by the lack of passion and deceit of others' excuses as to what was. My foundation was laid by two very young and immature people, I do not blame them as I know what 20-something mistakes look like, I have made more than my fair share. Yet, when the mistakes blossom into my destiny they could have been interpreted as life-changing but in all the wrong ways. It took quite some time but my perspective found fullness, realizing that my foundation could only be laid by myself. This revelation allows me the emotional self-control & security to know that my design is mine to own and the power in that is freedom.

Dear Diary,

Growing up is not easy and it is even more difficult when you have no example. Do you ever feel like you just throw some shit together and hope it comes out right? Well, that is me and I force the issue. This is what maturity and being a man looks like.

Yet in all honesty, I do not know. Me and my father well let us just say we share a face and name but outside of such, we are totally different yet ironically the same. My goal is to be better than I felt he was for me. Yet I feel I was born without a compass because he was not there for me. In my first fight I remember, a kid swinging and my first reaction was to weave and swing back. Luckily, I connected and he did not. So, my life has been a series of weaves and counters.

I remember our talk on the birds and the bees. It went like this, "hey here are some condoms make sure you wrap it up." I was a virgin at the time but had made Varsity Football so in his mind, sex was the next thing up for me. I went well over a year with almost 100 condoms and never even sniffed, felt, or interacted with a vagina. Funny how when I actually got to it, I was so eager to prove I was the man. I barely took into consideration the women I accumulated. Sex was more of a sport and definitely a form of frustration release or a reward for on-the-field accolades. It slowly became a hidden vice and discipline.

I took a lot from him through his mannerisms, my love for underground music, an insatiable desire for beautiful women, as well as hustle. Yet, I am quite certain where I got my work ethic, I am sure it was my mom as she worked every day of my life.

Like I said growing up is not easy not because to put it simply, most days, I just do not know how to or what it is I am missing or pursuing.

Today felt like:
"What's Next?"
Today's Questions:
"Where am I heading?"
"How do I get better?"

What is next, where am I heading, how do I get better, if it is a matter of self vs. external. My intentions had to be tempered, my patience had to be honed, and my discipline had to be defined. So, answering those questions, what is next is such a powerful question— myself, fatherhood, career while these are merely extensions of my answers. Moving forward is to understand where I fell short, embrace where I stepped up, and currently where I stand firm. Identifying that propels me to feats beyond material and worldly success, ones that elevate me to climb and expand. What is next is not GPS directions to a destination, it is a well-oiled machine running through a system—which is a proven method of success. Although I am broad in vernacular my contraction at times with words is the application —wild, explosive, compulsive, and described as mysterious. Life for me unfolds and as I experience it, I fully intend to learn it intimately along the way.

As with the foundation of any build a solid base is necessary to build upon, excavating the depths of myself and clearing residual karma and factors to first set myself up towards growth. Yet any build is meant to house more than merely oneself. That at best is ego looking to secure itself but dissolving that along with other facets, helps me to gain the beauty of every blessing this life holds, it also opens me to a solid place to rest it all upon. This is the first step and arguably the most important piece of diving into myself as a man and my soul.

GROUNDBREAKING

breaking new ground; innovative; pioneering.
new and likely[1] to have an effect[2] on how things are done in the future[3]:

Dear Diary,

Today I woke up in tears, I was flooded and dripping from my face uncontrollably. I had what seemed to be a beautiful dream and, in the end, was a mess of a nightmare. The trigger — the point with which erupted the barren space designed to be my pupils.

Today was something I had not experienced in over 2 years, since the passing of my great-grandmother. As I watched her lifeless body be carried out on a stretcher my heart and mouth aches and my eyes welled. Yet naturally, like almost any other time that I muster up enough emotion to cry, I retreat to do so alone. There have been rare occurrences where I was soothed and accompanied but if we are being honest that is few and far between.

Just like it has taken me years to cry, it has taken me years to destroy my entire paradigm. My self-esteem was a facade, my confidence merely a cover-up for a grown man with a shy boy complex. Unsure if I wanted to fully express my truths for fear of some invisible retaliation.

---

1. https://dictionary.cambridge.org/us/dictionary/english/likely
2. https://dictionary.cambridge.org/us/dictionary/english/effect
3. https://dictionary.cambridge.org/us/dictionary/english/future

I have not fully experienced myself, and honestly questioned why what happened to me has transpired. I simply endure it and figure that in some divine nature it means something. Like betrayal, hurt, and disappointment all mean I am mighty. While my ability to hold it in is a righteous means to show strength and divinity. Does my allowance of heinous treason and manipulation elevate me to new pinnacles?

My dream made me realize I am lonely, not miserable, or bitter, just simply lonely. I expect lies, and deceit, and I fill those voids with my imagination. My reality skewed to bend the laws of physics in favor of the space in which I can reside blissfully. My tears confirm that my self-doubt is as internal as it is perceived externally. My pain is deeply woven through the fibers of my being. I can dress it all up, and present it in a matter of self-assured bullshit but at the end of it all, it is deeply rooted insecurity. Hidden under my roots [a dead body], my dead body one that is as lifeless as my granny.

To add to matters I went and walked and it was a few degrees under chilly and barely above bitter. In my commute I shed more tears, realizing that my desires and wants are outside of myself. Yet ironically, I was again in the realization that I am alone and counting on another to trot in valiantly, is a mere fairy tale. A companion may be the very result of a beautifully written script, but I can only act it out, as it is great for the screen and ends once the credits roll. My eyes flooded and my face was wet from the thoughts of wanting to embody a beacon of unconditional love. I sometimes feel this world is so dangerously diseased that wellness and health are not what they seek but only mere destruction. I want to help the world more than I care to help myself and somehow that flaw has been the very part of me that has led me to the total destruction of myself.

I cried because I plan to show my children strength but I hide from my own Inner G. Today is not even halfway over and I have cried multiple times yet my body feels light. This level of vulnerability makes me feel less than others, it makes me feel as if I am unworthy.

But on this day,
I decided to turn my pain and tears into triumph. I decided to choose myself and do for others accordingly. Today I decided to be my own best friend and guess what?? I bet you I will not be lonely anymore...

At this stage in my life, growing was an uncomfortable must. We always discuss growing like it is this beautiful transition into a better self, when in all honesty it is painful, tiring, and trying. Growth is no more comforting than stagnation is progressive, just at some point, the discomfort is inspiration enough to continue onward. Sharing a piece of my emotions at one point felt dirty, like giving away that vulnerable space opened you to destruction and terror. People find it in them daily to use it either towards happiness or as a basis for sadness. Emotions were always fuel and more of an igniter than a steady stream of indicators, gentle nudges to course correct.

Emotions as a man are not a sentence to inadequacy, on the contrary they are beautiful reminders of humanity and passion. Guided by them should not be the goal but receptive and accepting of them as a step towards chiseling through things a material/practical viewpoint has limited access to. This day challenged even how I see my own humanity and emotional perspective. It wasn't pleasant but isn't the point of breaking ground meant to upend old forms and unnecessary objections?

Dear Diary,

I am fatigued and drained. I understand I am currently lost but why do I feel so assured. Why am I so calm? Is my life an illusion that allows me to exude bliss or is it an utter storm with which I find refuge in the eye?

Shit if I know, but more so than ever, I want to explore and travel and laugh and experience. Not remain confined. I want to climb mountains, soar over oceans, and relax under beautiful sunrises and sunsets. I am seeking inspiration, a zest, a zeal, something grandiose.

The kind of amazement that allows me to extract it from every fiber in my being. Shit if we are being honest. It is me, if I look in the mirror it is I. The thing I search for is to love so deeply. It is myself that I am searching for. The space with which I am in direct opposition.

Fuck that, fuck the expectation, forget the noise. I understand that I am the one. Something like a prophet more like an Oracle. Sadly, I knew this in my soul, I gave it away too easily. I shared it too much. Today I looked at myself like my soul is pure and fierce. Suddenly the coy demeanor turned into this flavor.

You know the one that smells delicious and tastes savory. Like you eat slowly just to make sure you did not miss a thing. Yeah, that is you, what the fuck were you worried about panting and panicking instead of removing who people told you "YOU" were AND being exactly who you are. Is it scary to be yourself…?

If so, suck that shit up…

Because you are definitely sculpting a work of art…

A block is put upon you to be removed and utilized all in one.

Impatience although is a trait of many, I had it bad and I do mean like right now. Not bratty but my impatience wanted to skip all steps, let us start and then finish. Constant setbacks, reevaluation, correction, stops, breaks, and all the process entailed did not excite me. As I write, format, edit, and pen this it creeps right back to say just finish already. Yet nothing in life merely appears. That is the confinement of living on this 3D planet in this space and time. So constructive thoughts, and refinement of experience, unveil the beauty of the whole and parts. It took a while but I got there. They say Patience is the greatest virtue because it tests your entire being. I can agree but one step further it builds you into the person you are to become behind it. These are questions I ponder on and thoughts that circulate.

If you were just given merely because you asked, what would alter who you are, so that you could receive it?

Dear Diary,

Last night I spoke about my traumas. Like my depths of pain, my illness that I have harbored deep in my being. My pain was expelled through conversation, my woes and worries worded so that they could be sonically ingested. It was therapeutic, which I am sure I needed and a big part of me wanted. I shared my mistakes and the decisions which have led to my rather mysterious demeanor. The reason why my voice sits idle in casual settings and my mind observes more than I would care to acknowledge. Shit in true form, my pain was relieved, it was revisited and registered an impulse in my mind. It was a throbbing sensor clearly blinking at where my isolation stems. The root of all my evil, the foundation of my mistrust.

I realized my mind and heart aged. My exterior is merely a boy but my internal functions light years beyond that of my peers. The halt of my growth was clipped, it was littered. It was sabotaged, and to this day I cannot fathom why those who said they cared for me would have done such. My only idea is that they possibly put and projected their limitations on me. Yet, deep down in my soul, I knew no fear was greater than I. My passion was derailed; my silence was written off as Submission and concession to faux friends, family, and feelings.

Fuck, last night was like surgery it was a disease being verbally emancipated from my being. I had to clearly view those who had damaged me internally, who severed my heart. I had to relive my pain.

It was as if the medicine I longed for was in the venom which had initially destroyed me...

Last night felt like alchemy...

If we as humans believed that we are original, nature would laugh. If we as men believe we are pioneering, then again nature would ask how? If we are in pursuit of what defines our own gifts, then GOD has a way of pointing us in that direction. If only we would embrace and accept it. Turning words into healing, love, passion, and growth may not be the salvation of the world but I promise your smiles & tears can both mend and build. That is to say, your gift is not in the vastness of your success or joy or dolled up through your pain and sorrow. No, your gift is wrapped into the very flesh you carry, the heart that beats, the mind that thinks, and the soul which carries the weight of it all. Take the time to believe you are as important as a drop in the ocean & equally as powerful as the entire ocean itself. Somewhere in there, you become something beyond your own imagination. I value my infinite possibilities paired with my finite existence.

It's the humble human paradox.

Dear Diary,

Yesterday I had a hell of a conversation. It included my deepest disappointments, my childhood trauma, frustration, and even the woes that readily rear their ugly head. Somehow my anger used to be fueled by a feeling of lack of importance, early obligation, and lack of creative outlet. My energy is beyond the average, my focus less than most, and my persistence beyond comprehension. My dedication is undying yet can be very messy and misunderstood. I would constantly go to battle and return severed, cut, bleeding, and gashed. Is that heart of a lion or ignorance and insanity at its highest degree?

I would place band aids on those wounds, expecting them to emotionally heal with no antiseptic or apology. It was a hole in my heart and it looked massive. Am I desensitized, no, am I scared of feeling deep down the joy of embrace?

I will answer that in my own due time.

Apparently, I carry my pain in the form of self-doubt, self-destruction, and deprecated talk. Therapy!? I may be beyond the point of reconciliation or merely at the demolition site of what my surroundings created for me to build upon.

Picture me rollin, on rollerblades, under the Santa Monica sunset.

No, scratch that, Montevideo waterfalls with nature adorning my flesh. Cleansing my woes, washing away my hurt, easing my pain. No longer accepting it and only utilizing pain towards goals that are necessary and worthwhile. I had put together soundtracks of relief and smoke blunts of enlightenment. That day, I will see the sunset as just another installation of myself and not the end. If it so happens to be the end, I will calmly accept that too.

Today felt like Change and a newfound direction!

It's been some time since I've expressed my thoughts and feelings. Yet I can sense an uprising.

I want to formally say Thank You. So many truths have found themselves in my lap. I've had old friends and family bring me so much information, wisdom, and clarity.

Knowledge has found itself in the same room as action and now it's greatly improved my vision.

Response and timing, technique and accuracy. I woke up one day and asked if I was cursed for not being able to shake my own dark clouds. I then realized that perhaps my clouds are not grey.

Perhaps my shine is hidden beyond the shadows I cover it with, could I possibly be the rain on my own parade?

LOCATION

I am not in balance with what I do and don't care for.

On one hand I want to be satisfied and at peace. I've learned to prioritize what's valuable and what is priceless. Different ideals and different people.

Yet what I found in my meditation today is that my identity has been warped around the concept of a partner or lack thereof. I slowed down and extended the bandwagon for what most would say is a foolish endeavor. Yet in my existence I enjoy the heroic battle of villain and protagonist. I so badly wanted to identify with the one who saves the day.

Yet nowadays I mimic the very destruction that lifts the veils of ignorance, that plagues those who I felt, knew better than I.

Numbing my very feelings with desensitized nonsense and safe havens like liquor, sex, porn, and denial. I've climbed into my grave and basically laid in the dirt and allowed others to cover me. Bury me by giving them my power. Given that I possess it, I've siphoned it to others and into others while I run in place.

I've been praying
I've been reading
I've been hoping
I've been vocal
I've been better
But the best is yet to come.
Yet Resilience is not equal to Resistance.
So let me EMBRACE ME!!!

Dear Diary,

Today I woke up at peace with the broken pieces. Oddly I was calm at the missed chances, excited by the failed attempts, and humbled by the lost acquaintances and loves.

It is not as if I never preferred those things at the point of transaction, do not confuse that notion with my fortified peace. It is simply finding joy in the journey. I set intentions to be and somehow the universe collided with me or colluded with me to see it through. The thoughts of people I once revered have quite metaphorically melted away. I utilize this self-teaching and pain to memorize myself better than any test or study guide, I learn myself. I find happiness in what is left and appreciation for what once was.

Today I believe I saw you and I do know it was not me being influenced.

Today Felt Like: finishing my first 5k, winded from the journey but proud of the ability to persevere it.

Today looked like Stained Glass beautifully broken yet adorned to a bigger picture.

The proximity of who we project to be, who we are, and what our true self needs can either crash from rigidity or align in true harmony. Many times, we fixate on who the world has told us to be, and what we idolize ourselves to be based on our surroundings, yet the power is in truly understanding ourselves intimately. If we were to sit with ourselves outside of our own bodies and readily embark on the journey to see ourselves whole, we could find where we truly sprout. The most difficult part is not finding ourselves, it is finding ourselves without the bias of others' perspectives. Empathy can be a gift but can also leave us halted as we have welded together so many varying visions of ourselves without first embracing the true intent of our own purpose. I found this road and path to be unsettling at first until I began to find my truest self, waiting to meet me as I grew to embrace, embody, and exude him as the man— I Am.

Dear Diary,

Today I cleaned myself not solely with just my external body but internally. Utilized my time to purge myself. I told someone I loved them because my heart needed to feel that presence of love that was unconditional. Not eating anything until after I left the gym and pushed myself even when I wanted to stop a set. I told some people I needed prayer because desperately I knew I could feel my spirit required assistance. I sent out apologies because I needed to truly feel forgiveness. I checked my own behavior and prayed. Then I cleaned my body and shaved. It all felt so small but important. I stripped my bedding and put on new sheets so that my dreams and rest can be renewed.

Today was transparent, I gave and did not feel taken advantage of. I simply gave away all that no longer served me. My attachment to old ways, people, items, and ideas. I cleared space for all that is new.

Today felt like: The first day of school.

New and unseen just being prepared to step out for the day.

Each step, the ones we have yet to take as men are a part of our purpose; some have the diligence to do the uncertain– others the passion to embark past comfort. The goal is one in the same to leave the mark that sits above and beyond yourself through yourself. These pieces of me are merely lived transcripts of what may be the very key to another's unlocked potential. Prepared by me but for the presentation of others– funny how life works in that way.

Dear Diary,

This morning was blissful, it was easy and so welcoming. I woke up on my own and rested well. My dream was a bit odd but I do not even understand it, so I will revisit it later. Anyway, today was like in the movie where the main character wakes up everything is damn near perfect. I mean, I looked to my right and nobody was in the bed with me. Yet my place was pristine and clean. Temperature relaxed and below my comforter was just me, no clothes, or restrictions simply loose. It had missing pieces so perfect by no means but more than average or tolerable. It was one of those days I had longed for, one that was without discomfort for the most part and introspective.

I calmly self-reflected, grabbed some literature, and found myself enhancing my mind. It was peaceful, to say the least, and a blessing to say the most. I sometimes wonder if who I am is enough or am worthy of the things I internally dream of. Am I doomed beyond repair because of past mishaps and what is my purpose on this plane? I spiritually seek enlightenment and even can glance back into my participation in Ramadan. In that season, I learned my fortitude and the truth of simplicity and sacrifice. Finding an understanding of why my circumstances were not my explicit choices but my universal decisions. Today things simply gravitated to me. The music spoke to me, passion ignited me, and purpose well it faintly was calling me. I am learning to tune into myself and like today, it is a beautiful masterpiece.

Today sounded like silence: powerfully empty yet available for numerous opportunities.

Reflection became the best way in which I could identify how aligned I was with myself and the focus of my next moment. Through carefully examining ways, mistakes, success, and identifying purpose it helped me to define myself further. It lets me be more discerning, more functional, and also more self-aware. Added time with myself wasn't the only goal but how I brought myself to those outside of me; paired with whom I found time to communicate with. This has been a lasting piece to growth as not only a man but as a spiritual presence.

Dear Diary,

Today was melancholy, yet I am feeling more and more empowered daily. I am claiming my abilities and diving into my greatness. It is freeing, so I am shedding things and ideologies that no longer fit. The rain finds me reflecting, listening to a few podcasts, and reading to find inspiration. Laughing to soften myself. Although today is calm it is a bit murky and the dirt is getting muddy. In that mud, I have to clean up some of the mess accrued and set boundaries.

It is actually relaxing to understand that my pain, darkest insecurities, and fears are readily available. I stare them in the face realizing that they only haunt me because I do not confront and stare them down. They only control me because I do not resume control of my own self and ability. Unwilling to believe in me even after the reaping of my rewards.

It is not by coincidence, I have subconsciously been affirming myself and suddenly my gravitational pull has attracted such a different spectrum of opportunity, abilities, and confidence. The rain used to be such a drag to me but today it felt erotic, sensual, deep, and passionate. I know it would have been better suited with a partner but currently, my focus is self-discovery and transformation. Constructively attacking myself. I feel reassured.

Building upon the growth of reflection then chiseling away at external sources of blockage and internal beliefs of limit, didn't initially pair well. It is difficult to sit down parts that you have carried for decades unknowingly and knowingly. It's almost subconscious and robotic where the motions feel rigid when breaking away from them. Not understanding that what is necessary for survival and what is mandatory for elevation do not usually mirror or they drastically contrast to a certain degree.

Location is standard but having clear direction can indicate where that location should reside. If I were to want to eat the options are abundant but if my direction is geared towards a specific cuisine then the steps and place I find myself are more clearly defined. In it location is not as important as what it shall provide, so as a child location meant– I want what I want. A momentary perspective, as a man I want what I deserve and require. Seemingly similar, it would seem as such wouldn't it? Then as the layers peel back and the vision clears the location becomes more clearly defined.

Standing at an elevated space removes lower insignificant pieces. As my location is significant only after I've decided my direction. So in essence— is a man's direction more valuable than his location?

The difference between a Master and Novice is experience, the difference between novelty and mediocrity is a lack of interest, the difference between mastery and mediocrity is the understanding of novelty in each experience. A master is no different than a student except he has spent more time with something past initial understanding. I plan to Master myself daily that will then point me in the correct direction. If and only then will my location be clear.

DESIGNS

Dear Diary,

    I promise I am trying to be my best; I am seeking my Zen, searching for my purpose. Yet for some odd reason, I never find balance. I seemingly fall as if I do not know the difference between my left and right. Am I that unbearable, do I seem to show people this image of foolishness? Yet ironically, it is one of those just keep pushing feelings but what am I pushing. My quiet responses leave me feeling trapped in a shell wanting to lash out but I always quietly retreat; as that rage does nothing for me mentally, emotionally, or physically. It only ages me quickly.

    I needed my Jazz today, I desired composure and elegance, and it brought me back down. I prayed numerous times and listened to my heartbeat. It was thudding so loud and seemingly I could hear, I was alive. Grateful for that reminder, I did my very best to change the perspective of my day. Today was not the most graceful, clear, or patient day but it surely was not the worst of them all. Today I survived the rain both metaphorically and literally. It was cold, damp, and somber. I was alone and truly enjoyed that part, for the company was the least of my worries.

    Today felt: deeply lonely and abandoned yet inwardly fulfilling.

Planning for bad days or accepting that they are what we make of them is a key component. Many times I wished and hoped for the best like this was some magical movie where all dreams come true. The folly in that notion is the reality by which we live is not centered around wishes and hopes rather concepts and designs. Even if abstract it most collectively works and for myself aesthetically brings me a sense of fulfillment. The reason jazz always centers me is that although it sounds sporadic and composed of chaos, because it is the beauty of life's variation in musical form. You need to start there because the worst has limits, the best is simply boundless.

Dear Diary,

Today was the residue of a high. A high of emotions, last night I performed competitively and lost gracefully. With humility I watched and awed those more skilled and adept at a craft, held in high esteem. Not performers but real-life poets, equipped with profound stories, vast vernaculars, and intricate themes and deliveries. It was merely music to my ears. I definitely was inspired. It felt so genuine and authentic like that hole-in-the-wall soul food or Mexican place. It was such a rewarding experience, it made me appreciate the new degree and the blessing of fatherhood, through the craft of wordsmithing. Along with that it evoked something I had been missing which was emotion, I felt the words and the messages, the plots were not scripted, not cloaked behind catchy punchlines, or masked by current events.

No these were real stories of pain, liberation, admiration, betrayal, disease, self-awareness, and most of all life. Not one artist made me feel anything less than genuine truth. The aftermath of that genuine truth was today as I raised and thought to myself about the workings of my evening. I then shifted to my current situation and quickly seemed to feel depressed, halted, and locked into the moment. I had the onset of a familiar feeling. My past was creeping up and letting me know that it had a lock on me. I began to have a brief panic attack.

Not at a steady pace but in racing out of time last minute make it happen do not fuck up because if you do you are going to be a failure and disappointment and you are too fucking old to be running all these thoughts together and not pausing to breathe and now you are exhausted, type of panic.

Just like that long run-on sentence, I was overwhelmed and stressed. This time for believing in a lie, and realizing that all that I could see were mistakes. Not opportunities, not chances to rebirth and resurgence. A place of inadequacy had a sign with my name and a table for one sitting right next to me. My mania was a familiar one.

The aftermath of the intimacy experienced last night was met...

With the feeling of destitution and loneliness...

At many times our focus is what determines our designs. In this moment only mistakes allowed me vision. Not growth, not experience, not depth, nor opportunity. We limit ourselves before we believe and know ourselves. Accepting confinement as truth to our ability, as the guide to our imagination, and the judge of our worth. Many times the frenzy of what could be is more daunting than the possible what couldn't be. I know this so well, and growing as a man required me to understand the latter to not be true and the former to be the focus of my journey towards truth. Once I captured the frenzy it sat there like an exhausted child no longer frantic but calm.

Dear Diary,

Today I vowed to implement a change, I looked myself in the soul and spoke to the little boy in my heart.

After admiring him I decided to join him on the playground, he had such a wonderful smile. A stranger was not something he had met but shy was definitely his initial delivery.

We ran, laughed, raced, and came up with games, literally turning nothing into everything. He was polite, pleasant, and jovial. With a grin, he asked me if I would come back again, maybe we could play football, or go swimming. So, I smirked but was delighted to tell him, yes, I will come back with those sounds nice. Fearlessly he lived, fell, got back up over and over, was outnumbered, and was smaller, yet none of those things seemed to play into his psyche. This little kid saw no obstacle he could not conquer.

My chest swells as I know this little boy so well, he is me and I am him.

Yet I forgot what he knew that was most important, things happen but how you respond lets you live in Heaven or Hell.

The one who saw the world as a playground. The one who lacked dissatisfaction, disappointment, and inner demons. The one who was bright-eyed and full of vigor, energy, and imagination. He was happy, he was okay, and the pain was but a temporary moment.

It began to get dark and his only disappointment was that he had to wait until light resumed to have this level of fun again. As I walked him home, he talked a lot, expressing his love for different people, places, and things. Not once complaining about his scraped knee or bloody elbow. He just spoke LOVE, and as we reached the place I remember distinctly.

He said if you are hungry, I will ask my mom if you can come in for dinner.

I kindly declined but told him to take care of his brother and love and protect his mother. That little boy gave me everything I already had.

So today, it felt like playing outside...

I understood at some point manhood would have to clear the childhood messes I made. The ways I faltered, the fears I carried and the habits I justified it all with. This in itself made me see my child-like self in a problematic way, then suddenly I remembered what the mess was, it was art. Drawing a stick figure family on our walls, to the adult mind I made a mistake but to me, I expressed myself, the best way I knew how. The interpretation of my light shines through in each little occurrence but patience and pride run thin & thick in adults where the opposite should hold true. Where do you find time to sit with the possibility that these expressions stifle who you become as a man. My messes began to become masterpieces and my manhood was not some steady fault of disappointment but a reevaluation of what matters. Who Am I? A great question—a better one.

Am I who I am?

This one– not only questions me to understand my design but to question my design of myself. In truth to things, I cannot clean up, modify, or fix. It asks myself if I am being true to myself and not the expectation of others even amid their expectations. In due time — as for now I continue on.

Dear Diary,

Frustration may be an understatement, not exactly sure how to alleviate it. Wondering how on earth I had allowed myself to fall for this same trap. It is not as if I have not bumped my head enough. It is more like I decided to continually touch the hot stove after being burnt. I can blame no other as it is quite possible, masochistic how I behave.

I am calmly upset, not loud and boisterous but silently bothered. Not phased or thrown off but surely not in any mood to be occupied with another's company. I typically find solitude in music but I am now attempting to not just find slumber as my escape. Tonight, I will find inner peace. I have been working towards a better me.

Today felt like: "Let's Sleep on It and Try tomorrow!"

CONSTRUCTION

Dear Diary,

    Today I had a light conversation with my brother. We kind of just had small banter not as strong as our conversation has been as of late. Yet it was one of those I am grateful for this type of moment. I found beauty in something money could not buy and the media could not portray and that is quality time. You cannot quantify that in any form of tangible currency it is only exchanged in true love. We discussed relationships but I will save that for another time.

    Well after that conversation I met a young man who was seeking a progression. I held a small dialogue; I pray he becomes a success in whatever light that he is supposed to shine. After which I took a walk and watched the sunrise.

    Then my mother and I had a talk over breakfast, my mother is of another caliber. But if you have ever met her, you realize just how deep her impact reaches. Anyway, so we then ran some errands and just discussed things.

    My day was one I overall appreciated.

    Today was insightful, reflective, and most of all an amazing day. I can say that love is an ever-changing thing.

    Today was beautiful.

    It felt like the perfect Sunday in Fall...

In meeting humans, a rule is people matter so much —the ones who made life possible for you have something special to give you. It is only right that my manhood is tested and understood in the polarity of the woman who first granted me life. She may never know how to teach me to shave or what manhood fully embodies but her being a woman, shows me I can define what being a man is. She came from a time of change, a futuristic space that was foreign and that would someday be the present. She carried her past but always saw toward her future, she knew that more was to come. So, in that space she showed me what was behind me can stay put, what is in front of me is to be decided upon, but today is the moment I get to live in. Manhood is subjective in many formats, it is a blessing, responsibility, and privilege. It is an armor to be worn honorably to protect her womanhood which in its fullness came down to something so simple —her expression and choice of it. Thank You for always being unique. It lets me be the same—no limitations necessary.

Dear Diary,

Today was drowsy, almost depressing and reality escaping. I used so many different thoughts and emotions today. Like the ones you have to look up, to even understand it is a fucking feeling in the first place. It was a reminder, a crisp smack not like a delicious kiss on the sharp smack of truth. It was not frightening but more so jolting. Apparently, it is not an unfamiliar place now that I recall. I mean I have had days like this before. It was my reaction that took me exactly to where I needed to be. My attitude led me to either salvation or destruction. Ultimately, I chose success. At least this time. Yet it had not dawned on me that was my goal. I defined love and home. I revisited purpose and passion. Somehow things are not meek. They graduated to preciseness, a roar and rumble, and a soar. Today was like a rainy day with beautiful music. It seemed to flow like waves. Steady and distinct, consistently changing and rippling. Today was a place of happiness wrapped up in a high space of uncertainty. I could imagine this is the exhilarating feeling of skydiving. A cleanse of sorts is a distinct truth of separation.

Today felt cleansed and clear. Fresh and beautiful!

A choice comes with response and resistance, mainly resistance is the opposite factor. Changing my diet came with withdrawal from certain pleasures and cravings, and fitness came with the resistance of a bit more rest or idle activities. So, the choice or decision to do one will always release the other option. As a man navigating, my eyes are easy and simple but enforcing my "NO" is problematic, difficult, and sometimes a sacrifice. Few actually care and most do not but the pathway to a bigger and more divine purpose is nestled in those choices. Some are also made for us once our intentions have been decided. You have to release things to receive others. God and Life, give and take—although we find one to be positive and the other negative, manhood has taught me neutrality. My choices are now a bit more intuitive and higher-self guided not ego-driven; I still struggle at times but perhaps that is my own resistance.

Dear Diary,

For the last 3 nights, I have awakened to a lack of oxygen, almost as to indicate sickness but more so closer to a feeling of death. I find myself filled with congestion, yet water does not subside and at the final completion of mucus removal, I find my mouth to be barren & sore. I cannot pinpoint the reason; I have been active but can say I have also dabbled in guilty pleasures but I feel helpless. Unfortunately, nobody is here to save the day except me. I constantly battle with this level of self-destruction. In battle, I constantly spar within myself. Bustling for possible success and distinct position. My mind slowly digests my thoughts and utilizes them as a response. Pushing forward not truly because I want to fully but more so because I have an obligation to. My mind will not fail me as it has done in the past. My voice shall not quiver or remain silent as it has in the past.

I ……

I am not a victim; I am a victor. Victors find a way, and victims find an excuse. What am I finding?

Dear Diary,

I am in a season, one of ingenuity and ingestion. Equally, I am in a high influx of expression and creation. It is like I take in and give out. I summon research and actively create and materialize those findings. It may be a higher state of mind. Today is pressing, a pressure I know all too familiar yet my attentive calm nature is for some reason remaining strong and active. Viewing life in a variety of possibilities. It is like a Buffett and naturally, I can gather any variable combination but precisely I diagnose my highest desires and also my trivial wants. It is like life teaching me to feast yet gradually and remember that I can come back. More are available and welcome to my return.

Today was like clay work. Imagination paired with material and sealed in a furnace then to the kiln...

Building manhood is a process, not quite a finish line more so a redefined version that never quite is set. As it progresses through life goals, milestones, changes, and moments in time.

Dear Diary,

I shed my shield today and removed my armor. I exposed myself, loved myself heavily, and even decided that being vulnerable was a blessing. I understand this quote better than ever now.

"Life is a balance of letting go and holding on." -Rumi

I was harboring feelings. I walked yesterday and it was at least 3 or 4 Miles and, in that trek, I discovered my inner workings and demons. I realized I was holding onto pain and deceit. My soul was still in turmoil. No matter how clean the appearance was and how much I had cleaned things up. Underneath it, all was a trembling and damaged foundation. It was built upon false pretense, lies, and my blind faith and optimism. It made me hold onto deception and disappointment.

Unfortunately, the longer I held the more covert it became. Manifesting in finances, romance, and even overall wellness. I was believing that who I am and what I am destined for was this abyss of despair and misery. I had been blending and culminating synergies with others of wrath and internal self-destruction. I was fighting myself like many others around me.

Not understanding that they too were dealing with pain, they were filled with doubt, they too had tough moments in which fear depressed them. No matter how sweet the exterior was, that internal clock was not correctly wound up. I am now transmuting that energy and realizing it for what it truly was, a test of faith, boundaries, and love. A moment of realization and resilience. Those doors that were not opened, those relationships that fell through, those opportunities that were dead ends. I see they have all brought me higher. It is not easy to do that maintenance and deep clean but it definitely is worth it.

Today felt like a detox...

Ironclad discipline is difficult, it lacks excitement paired with the mundane tedious task. Over-indulgence is a snowball that easily can avalanche yet the middle ground is even more dangerous disciplined indulgence and impulsive behavior has the consistency of discipline with the detriment of over-indulgent behavior it slips us into an addictive space, while for some it is passed down through repetitive grooming from family or societal situations. In the grasp of it, you first have to be honest with yourself and detox all the lies. Share your darkness and turn the venom into medicine.

Dear Diary,

Last night was useful, and this morning meaningful and insightful. Yes, it definitely was that sort of transaction one that leads to deep introspection. How vivid things start to become, it is like roadblocks are easily noticed and solutions simply manifest. Yesterday I grabbed some new lenses. I have decided to self-care myself and love myself first. Unfortunately, that comes at the expense of losing those whose only intent is to use your care and wisdom for themselves. I am at a place of calmness. My piece describes it for the most part with a few omissions (Calm) . It truly is a testament to my genuine feelings concerning my path. Things will always be turbulent; it is the means to prosperity and growth. The soil must be broken to plant and grow. While, I simply look myself in the face and now my animal ambitions have slowly leaked into an unforgettable and rare aura. The fact of the matter is this version of my being has always been readily accessible but it needed to be honed. A severance, the irony that it included being the person that I have been but most never understood including myself. So those who were either aware or as confused as me no longer hold value. Well possibly...

Today felt like a new upgrade...

DEVELOPMENT

I weep not because I'm scared, no fear is the last emotion that comes to mind.
I weep at destruction, hurt, pain, and evil.
Since I was young this world seems upside down.
There could be many worldly reasons.
1) I'm a lefty (so minority)
2) My skin is colored (people of minority)
3) I'm a Male + #2
4) I adore Women who fall into any category of #2
How do any of these turn my world upside down? Not quite sure? I just know I've felt my share of pain, hurt, disrespect, neglect, and disappointment.
I've heard NO many times when YES should have been the only answer.
I've also heard YES which leads to a barrage of excuses as to why the YES never happened. When I would have fared better with NO.
I watched DEATH after DEATH, natural and un. While ingesting fear, sorrow, agony, disadvantage, and insecurity.
I have tried my best to be all that they say you should to succeed. I've bled, cried, and sweat to see better than what I was constantly given.
Then I was left by myself to figure it out.
Then I was told to step back to let others go ahead.
Then I was directed to an alternate route.
Then I was stripped of my sight so I couldn't see clearly.
Then I was told to WIN AT ALL COST.
But this was once the game had already begun.
2020 has been my life in live action. It has been the world I've always seen. Unsettling, unnerving, unfair, cruel, and selfish.
Yet what I've learned myself is to find what makes your world better and pass that light to those around. I stopped looking to those who cared or didn't

care long ago. Not because this world could harm me, but because of what Healing I could bring to it.

So if you feel disenfranchised, overwhelmed, hurt, broken, tired, or just overall scared.

Find YOUR PEACE...
Find YOUR LOVE...
But above all ELSE...
Be willing to PROTECT IT AT ALL COST!!!

Dear Diary,

Life is not easy currently, it is actually quite uncertain. Yet in my moments of patience, I have filled it with fellowship. In the past few months, I have performed a few times, begun attending bible study, and frequent a meditation group. These forms of expression have removed me from the fear of destruction. My incessant belief is that what I have worked my ass off to have success be stripped away, that I am somehow unworthy of a blessing. That I should live in turmoil due to my mistakes and shortcomings of past transgressions. I believe that my circumstances have shown me to remain confident in even the bleakest moments that my quiet mind and sure heart will supersede any mere idea of unworthiness.

Every time the unknown arises, somehow God is in the dark maneuvering through the trenches. I have actually had a turbulent relationship with life and the issues I have encountered have sometimes held me hostage. Today I am breaking through my own obstacles and challenges effortlessly as if they are my zone of comfort. My passion has me leaping through situations that before would literally have me down and out. I am assured in myself and realize that I will continue to be tested. My integrity and spirit are at peace... even in the midst of uncertainty.

Today I felt anointed...

I figured coming to the table as a fractured man or adult would lessen me, how could I live up to the expectations? Where do I fit in the scheme of what this is? I am grateful for New Deal & Rahel Daniels, surely that group and this person know maybe only a fraction of their importance but I was accepted even if only for a moment as someone to be cared for and considerate of. I can never thank all that I was given and hopefully left; it was a community of exactly what I needed most from those I knew little to nothing about.

Dear Diary,

Today was well thought out, it was a test and, in all honesty, I am glad it was. Today I caught nuances and paid attention to body language and people's level of purpose. I can truly say that I was present, it was quite apparent that what was in front of me was myself and the version of myself. It was the older version, the one that was outdated, broken, and non-functional. The new me was uploading and it was slowly upgrading and that upgrade is so amazing and not even completed.

I would easily go on and on about this but today was definitely a level-up...

Leveling Up is not the goal or prize but a gentle pat on the back that means you are still here and making progress.

Dear Diary,

As I sip and soak, my body shivers not from chills but due to the agitation my soul and patience my mind and body are currently undergoing. God has not failed so my assurance in the work is one of an unwavering faith. Identifying this chill as one of change, one that has had me test the depths of myself to find love in & all around me whilst I water, cultivate, nourish, and grow it. Before, I had been greedy, self-serving, and prideful. Believing that I was the only gift God blessed this world with as if my presence was not to be matched. Wild thoughts I know, it was downright narcissistic at times and on its calmest days quietly arrogant. Not giving the glory of my ability to prepare and be who I am due to God's Grace & Mercy.

Humility has found that in my heart and soul, answers are tucked away and God's blessings are never out of reach. Ascension, Elevation, and all the other fancy synonyms for doing better cannot really define this alignment. For years I have studied spiritual practices. Religion, chakras, tantra, Taoism, Buddhism, Astrology, Crystals, and many esoteric forms of therapy. Yet at the distinct root, it was calling for me to find my eye in the storm, my patience, my calm.

Speaking gently to those that I previously viewed as a threat has unlocked far more than my brash and brawny approach of the past. My smile has found its authenticity, and graciously enough my heart has lightened. Not seeking to please the outward expectations but listening to the Godly voice deeply tucked underneath all the noise of life.

My test has shown me that much is out of my control and even more so that my voice can speak the truth and not be accepted. My thoughts to enlighten the world are simply a constant conversation with myself about my own value and self-esteem.

No amount of settling, no degree of accomplishment, or a drip of sweat can exemplify it if internally it is lost. My accolades, although worldly, are mere placeholders where one day they will be rewritten in another's name. My possession and grasp of someone are not only a futile belief but one of egotistical deceit. I cannot hold or be held hostage. I have to love and live. Bless and be blessed. Give and be given the joy of that gesture. Otherwise, my actions are in vain.

I pray that I am not ahead of myself and am merely walking the path God has designed for me. Yet, in any stature, I do believe that I am truly tapping into the vessel of my purpose, something that I before had not even acknowledged I lacked. I identify my weaknesses and turn them swiftly into my place of study, healing, and practice. Consistently challenging an unknown opponent.

You ever study, take a test, then as you turn it in it feels like you missed nothing. Then when it was returned to you, even if you did not get a perfect score, you ACED it.

Today felt sort of like that!

A quiet accomplishment and humble happiness!

Thank You, God!

Dear Diary,

I sit here bare, not literally bare, oddly the chill from the room and window has me shivering. Cold and weary, I am seeking heat and warmth. Refuge and safety. Remaining calm amidst the harsh realities, I allow emotions to run through me. I am bare, ready to attack and charge ahead, available to possibilities and the vast universe. I believe that I can overcome my circumstances and this would literally be the portion in which I ceded first. Nope, not this time. I am moving, charging ahead, and ensuring along the way I remain humble. My heart was steady, my knees fortified, and my mind adept and malleable. I sit here with nothing to cloak me, no smoke to cover me, no mirror to trick me.

I am in faith, patience, and execution mode. My aims are set and I am shooting for Pluto, Sirius A, and beyond the current Galaxy. My abundance is otherworldly, I just know that somehow mediocrity is not for me.

Seeing myself bare and knowing that I can make these wonderful, beautiful, and magnanimous things manifest.

Let me know the chill and frigid can only stop those who let it!

Dear Diary,

I am not sure if I say this often but for some reason, I feel in a zone of extreme GREATNESS. Nothing can touch me, nothing is startling me, my mind and body are adept and my spirit is strong. It has been a while since this trinity wrapped itself and intertwined effectively. I know it is genuine because I am currently a magnet. I am attractive, not in the sense of physical appearance although if I would say so myself a brother-looking might-t-FINE.

No, seriously I am like this level of attraction that is almost scary, I can cut through the bullshit and I see heaven and opportunity everywhere. I am not desperate, my mind is sharp, my body solid, my heart is healing, and my spirit resonates.

In all honesty, right now things are not how I desire them to be, I would love to truly say that I have everything I want. Yet mercy and grace have given me all I need. I realize that not only am I aware of this but others are keenly aware too. Yet, I will keep quiet and utilize this momentum and continue. Inertia is the hardest to overcome but kinetic energy is the one that allows you to power through.

Right now, I am utilizing my kinetic energy, today felt like greatness in motion!!

Those subtle moments, the ones that show progress and progression in unison are simple reminders that it is all worth it. When darkness, sacrifice, tears, and so many other sides of pain creep into your space the slither of a glimmering light is enough to know that you are balanced and that healing is coming. Failure is a necessary part of the process into greatness, once you *are in* motion the obstacles are no longer that but merely additions to your greatest version.

The cross of manhood for myself is one of submission:

The moment my cross came to me was difficult. David was not prepared to slay the Giant Goliath. What he had was enough preparation. He submitted his notion that it was impossible and accepted the problem of the entire village.

As a pretense to the thought and wave pattern, I am in tonight. This episode is brought to you by PTSD and Courage.

Trusting fear is something I am faced with daily and sometimes my pride made me feel I was docile or meek and sometimes I honestly was. Other times my pride did not allow me to be my very best. I have been dishonest with myself. Yet the one thing I realized is the true severity of instances. Although I was risk ready, I always had a mature caution on the limit I would extend. I placed my ceiling so low I never made it out of my own basement. Now as an adult my apprehensions have become one of habit. I battle with my own actions like I am tussling with myself. Now a days I move forward and now I seem to treat obstacles with a smirk and mental fuck you. Yet sometimes my emotions and an inner voice cry for a long boisterous roar or a grand gesture to show the world I have won. Yet results speak louder than words. It is ok to be loud but I care more to be received than just seen as a loud gesture. I needed to shed the experience and expectations. I am currently fasting. It is Ramadan and I am observing because somewhere along the way I wanted to find my own place and identity.

Dear Diary,

Today I woke up not depressed or oppressed simply just in the presence of somber thoughts. I did my daily routine, thanked God for breathing and another day and asked my daily question. "What is my purpose!"

Please take pity on me as I've somehow managed to ride the wave of 27 years and feel utterly lost. Is this exactly what I should feel? Numb downtrodden, undoubtedly empty, but endlessly realistic while vaguely optimistic.

Do my words, touch souls, fulfill roles, or slowly drop ink onto pages like erratic raindrops amongst the window pane. Fuck helping others, I need to help myself, free my own demons and let the bastards roam free.

Sex and alcohol find comfort atop my lips, the precipice of my dick shattering the depth of her hips. Am I unholy or vile for viewing life in a series of ins and outs and moans and pants? I ask for forgiveness and embark on sin once more, is this something I enjoy in the form of Stockholm, it holds me hostage.

Today I feel somber and yet with a level of appreciation and gratitude, I send out love in the same thread I sent out explicit joys. Funny how it all flips. One day we are just friends and the next we have a deep conversation that ends with my mouth on your tits, tongue on your clit, breathing down your spine and one candle stays lit.

That was simply my imagination running wild, somehow you fit the description. Yes, you are not the vixen who is dolled and animated, no you with the stretch marks and areas you feel are unworthy to see the light of day. The very dark spaces let me know you are real, in this artificial social scene. Those marks and blemishes cannot be angled away. The very shape that cannot be hidden once unwrapped from a long day.

Back to reality, I am chasing masculinity but not the kind they say is toxic but the BIG DICK ENERGY, which gravitates around me like an everlasting aura. Is it money, is it cars, charisma, or my fashion. My confidence hung on the thin veil of external value and constantly conflicted with internal morals. My real world seems to be never-ending strife so no wonder I jump back into my imagination, for in it I make all the rules. Yet the reality is a hard pill to swallow. I swore I took the red pill but maybe my reality has left me color-blind. I will try again tomorrow.

"What is My Purpose"

I falter and still look to challenge my own self-awareness and esteem.

So now I want to Carry my cross. It is mine to bear and I will dump off all unnecessary baggage.

Fasting is a form of detox and release. It is a deliberate action intended to provide inactivity to problems.

So, although there are many around me, I must work on my best. That day is daily.

My cross to bear....

INNOVATION

 I don't particularly care for sequels. Never really seen a good one if the original is a classic the follow up always fails to compare. So I'm sitting here thinking. Why am I stressing over past relationships, past mistakes, past decisions, and possible rekindled moods?

 Today isn't more so a toll on my esteem as it is my existence. Teetering between am I doing enough and what tf am I not doing that I should be. I chastise myself and then remember I have to be strong. Absent minded won't unleash my true gifts, my intellect. I mean I'm no slouch but my mind is an endless abyss that can generate greatness or fold me into inadequacy. My mind is limitless but this world is finite and for that I have to remember that others are as well. My vessel is temporary and my moments dissolved along the path. My ego is loud today and my self awareness is allowing it to simmer down.

 I just know that many things I've had before none of them appeal in today's world. So I'll focus on the moments at hand and am glad for what's moving forward.

 LIFE

Dear Diary,

 Today I am at a crossroads, merely learning from past experiences and growing through new challenges. I am thankful for what I have accumulated more-so wisdom than material possessions, the turmoil has led me to a sense of sacred Zen. I have discussed this before so I will halt that portion. Yet I wanted to make known those whom I am appreciative of not merely for anything that they have done externally but for the ways they poured into me internally. My tribe has grown, my vision focused, and my thoughts a bit less cloudy. Yet challenges are on my horizon. As I currently write this my unsure nature is not to overshadow my faith but it equates that I am heading into the unforeseen yet memorable territory. This is no foolish means of psycho-seasoning or trick towards logical thinking of what lies ahead. I shall find my calm, my comfort, and my decision to persevere is one that I confidently accept! No steps back...

Diary I will be back but for right now...

I will SUCCEED!

I remember as an athlete those tiring reps, going again & again past the point of exhaustion. While those particularly tough practices and recovery days never brought me physical comfort, come game, or meet day, my prepared abilities made it all worth it. Some days I say sign me up when it comes to the grueling truth that is my own greatness. Yet, on those days where before exhaustion can even creep into the vicinity my psyche and soul have to persevere through. Yes, sounds like some movie triumph story but some days it is getting up and making it happen and not knowing when it will end just to tire out and do it all again. It is lonely, it is unsure, but just like those excruciating moments as an athlete, IT CAN'T LAST FOREVER! I am SUCCESS and I honor every bit of it!

Dear Diary,

The actual date I will not disclose but it is Sunday, today has been a series of highs and lows per usual and I can say my patience is being tested. Yet my harvest is slowly coming in, I am doing silent work. The kind that is delicately disguised and ever so effortlessly undetectable. Not in a form of manipulation or deception but of higher blessings. It felt good today and I received the Love I needed in the perfect way.

Keep It Simple. Never forget as you grow things must be released and let go....

growth is making way for new opportunities, clearing debris, navigating uncharted paths with tested methods and being flexible to adapt. Keeping it simple is no more a saying as it is a lifestyle. This does not mean be ambitious or have grand ideas, it means don't fluff what isn't necessary.

Dear Diary,

I have woken up after little to no sleep, I have missed quality time with my daughter and this circumstance is not ideal or wanted. A fucked-Up sacrifice & hurtful at that. I know that it will not be forever but this is not it. This is not how I envisioned it. Well, the goal is to set the intentions decided. The next step is belief and action. I cannot sit and think think think think think think think. I have to pull up my dreams and live in them. So I am in a new mode, it feels awkward but necessary. I will not apologize for either because I am not really sorry. Those that I love will surely understand because they will be in attendance and reap the love and growth of it. I am indestructible, I have seen God has hardened me, not maliciously but for war with what I had to accept. It was not always glorious, it sometimes was tough and I wanted to quit, give up and stop. That is not an option. Rest is necessary. I know that now but I also know that I do not have to play their game but I can surely dominate it. I am done being Meek.

Today was a mixture of purpose & GODconfidence.

At some point your innovation comes to you, your mind and heart are equally magnetic. If you are truly pursuing the purpose, the doors and help needed to succeed wants you as equally as you want it!

In my journey of manhood, the realization I had to accept is not apologizing for my manhood. My imposition of another reality or experience is only based on relativity to circumstance. When a team wins the World Series do they apologize for winning or that a team lost a player due to injury, NO. Why, because as it turns out the only things in my control are my expression of manhood and how that aligns with my responsibilities and priorities. God has blessed me and if I spend most of my time apologizing to those who do not care to accept their own truth is not my problem or concern. Brazen in many ways and polite in many more, I seek success to achieve such being present in my reality. PURPOSE embodies me and GOD fuels me.

Dear Diary,

Something in me has two very conflicting views, yet my mind is calm, slowly reminding me of consciousness. My understanding of myself is growing. I have ingested the world and the taste has many flavors. Yet I am indulging in my own pot. Brewing myself and engulfing myself in my scents, intimately finding new ways to arouse my own mental collaborations with my heart teaching me self-love. I believe that loving yourself deeper comes at the expense of those who only knew you for shallow purposes. The depths of my soul are now my resting grounds. The places many shy away from, the darkness and light buried deep within. My God has led me to find lessons in troubles, kindness in pain, and purpose in uncertainty. I listen to patience in times of flustering events, gradually discerning between wants, necessities, blessings, and mercy. Control, something I seemed to feel I could contain has been removed from my grind. I only control myself. Maneuver through my own mess, clean up my own thoughts, and organize my own chaos. I literally stand as a tribute to a pillar.

It all ends but before the change can take place, I must start the process.

As I have stated, the process at a juncture was not my favorite part. The work I did not mind so once my head was down, hey I could work until no more is left. Yet that is not sustainable in building masterful and great feats. It is not a one-day push or two-week sprint. It is a mile-by-mile marathon, with tempo, pace, direction, vision, and coordination to be navigated to a destination. Piece by piece, so accepting this unsettling and uncomfortable truth was the beginning of my process of manhood.

Dear Diary,

Today I had to sacrifice, I had to let go, I had to have a temporary casualty and it inflicted my own heart. It hurt me to hurt one whom I love. It bothered me to leave someone whom I desired to be in my presence. I shed tears and seemingly the pattern of last year's innate ability to feel openly and expressively has undoubtedly seeped into this year as well. Not ashamed of it, nor emasculated from it. I feel myself overcoming and overpowering my ego. As it merely is not by chance that this is merely a newfound level of depth and emotional expression. My life has been very low and exponentially high. Yet today my tears were not alone, they were not only mining my heart they were one whom I love, one who melts my entire being. So today was a test, one that I cannot merely take lightly. My life seems to be crumbling before my eyes yet it somehow is the demolition of the false teachings and ways that had enslaved me in a place that was not merely designed for me. I love the world and today, I felt love in pain. Although a tough lesson to learn, it made for an even tougher one to teach. Yet absence makes the heart grow fonder. So, until next time...

If I allowed my emotions to guide me, I would drown. I utilize them to my advantage, and I can venture into the world and beyond. I rather the latter than the former.

Dear Diary,

Today I was exhausted, not exactly sure why my energy level was so low but I can take a surefire guess. Things have been rather difficult here as of late, in almost every way imaginable but I seek to find various spots of gratitude and abundance. It may seem redundant but honestly, it may be the one thing that is keeping me from sinking into a place of depression that I fought for years to shovel myself out of. I know that somehow and someday things will grow from this difficult time, as for now, I am remaining faithful & patient. Otherwise today I finished a very insightful and highly recommended piece of literature. 9 Steps to Financial Freedom by Suzan Orman. Now not to say I finished all 330 pages in merely a day but today I completed my last 65 or so pages and honestly it ended completely differently than expected. I have a few other books I am currently finishing up as well. On my challenge to finish 36 or 3 a month by my birthday. Yet I am several books behind my desired pace. Anyhow, today I felt weighed down. I miss my children and for the first time in quite some time, I actually crave a deep and close intimate relationship. I will chalk it up to gloomy weather but something in me today saw my value and realized I deserve to be loved and love someone as equally deserving. In essence, I think I was wishing to have someone to simply be with at my current time. I swiftly snapped out of it and realized I do not need nor am I positioned to take on the responsibility of another's well-being as I am currently building my own.

Yeah, today was draining but I got up, made myself dinner, and took a long bath. So maybe I need to replenish and wash away all the problems.

Self-care is such an overused term, yet caring for our own overall being is top-tier and important.

Dear Diary,

It is a bit uncomfortable setting certain boundaries I must admit. Like it is tough to acknowledge that sometimes I am not as interested as I am putting on to be. That what I am looking for is something that takes time and patience and I always feel as if I lack both. I am not going to allow pessimism and doubt to creep into my head. It is at this familiar crossroad and I am tempted with old pleasantries and I have come to a vast understanding of what I NEED to be, who I am and want to be. It is not loud or obnoxious nor is it boisterous. It is silent and diligent. I remember that I was not a jester merely jovial and I was not a fool merely naive & observant. I love to spot things and utilize them. I am a problem you would care not to have and a blessing you wish would stroll your way. I am not in control anymore and that is fine. I relinquished that subtly unrealistic request. As I understand it there are numerous variables. So, I am simply going to embrace, enjoy, and learn. I am actually nervous but excited about the ride.

Today felt like letting go...

As you build projects, relationships, ideas, families, and life. The only sure constant is an end and release so that things can become new. Never be afraid to let go!

The concept of an element of success is along the way, not those who do not value and or understand you! It aligns with obstacles, failures, and mistakes along the way. Boundaries are defined as a wall or divider instead they should more be a tollway, infrastructure, or vessel with which your greatness lies. Manhood and being handy but living in a space where nothing needs attention then show your own lack in that space. Creating boundaries and environments where we thrive, understanding our seasonal strengths and weaknesses. Where to pivot and place yourself is about the best and highest form of control you possess. The free will, yet so many other factors

Control is a learned concept, we learn it subconsciously through those who without accepting their lack of control, push the idea of being in control of others. Self-control as a man is a sword used to discipline one's self from peril and defeat but also a guiding weapon to forge new paths and unlock vast possibilities.

RESISTANCE

Addiction and Depression are very real and very cunning.
My first stint with my depression seemed to be a never ending woe. I mean a constant feeling of isolation, unacceptable behavior, and a continuous circle of settling for less. This then brings me to the world and how my past haunts my future greatness.
Like I'm stumbling over failed circumstances, lost acquaintances, and empty promises. Self Sabotage is playing line leader to stress, validation seeking, and actions that harm. Oh let's not forget the daily serving of anxiety, guilt, and shame.
Self Judgment is the only thing that can save me.
But I was subconsciously taught that as a black man, even the innocent acts can result in destruction. So if I flip the coin properly it always lands GUILTY.

So now my mind is treating myself with the self respect society polarized in my image as I don't seem to quite fit this norm. So my radical ways leave me as a lonely wander searching for balance.

Life still goes on....

Yes that was a brief intermission that you must decide and do so with haste as no time is available past this moment which if you waste could turn into you running yourself in circles deciding what way is up when the next turn is in 7.9 miles heading southwest at 45mph.

Oh hello ADHD nice to see you old friend. I mean focus is such a tough task already why not add more onto my plate.

So as clarity comes along....

I question what exactly am I addicted to and what has me truly feeling defeated.

Saddest part is most times it's just me myself and I
Trying to figure out where I went wrong.
Or plot twist
What I've learned and what is to come.
To Be Continued...

Dear Diary,

I can feel the pressure and the magic today. I can see that there are limitless possibilities and an abundance of blessings. If only your eye can see, pursue, and encompass them. I know that what is going to happen may not be to my utmost approval but will be to my utmost salvation. Yet I have come to terms with the fact that I do not know what tomorrow brings. That being given is not a curse and it is a gift that God has blessed me with. I am also sure that what will be will be. I have panicked on past occasions out of fear and control. Yet today as cold and lonely as it is, I am seeking and finding various forms of warmth. I have found a healthy community, negated ideas that would not be suitable for my talents and gifts, and also have found ways to grow through pain, uncertainty, and the obstacles that typically I am confronted with. I am affirming so many different things and doing them silently. As loud and boisterous announcements are merely ways to seek attention that will not compensate for hard work, persistence, and dedication. I am not buckling and although the process is not to my exact liking it is one of the Humble proportions. In that, I see or feel that I am in more clarity but I will reflect and continue praying about such! In the meantime, I have to continue because more has to be accomplished but it has to be purposeful. I may just be onto something.

    Today feels fulfilling...

Although rewards are beautiful, the service that comes from them is just as fulfilling. Knowing the overflow of fulfillment comes in multiple forms and many times the destination or the award or degree seems as the focal point. Yet that feeling of seeing your expression and helping build up another is the fulfillment of service, while one is emotionally and ego-driven for our own adornment. The latter is a transfer of your service and gifts and in return not a monetary but a fulfilling currency is returned. It governs us, then as we decide what we want out of life we can build towards success which is how we as men can build up a better world. Yet before looking towards the destination, decide what I want so it guides me towards a service that provides universal fulfillment, in that road and path I walk towards my goal, and rewards are presented. This cycle eluded me in my youth as my experience expanded, and my understanding of this has attracted success. It is fulfilling beyond merely myself.

Dear Diary,

Not that I believe this to be some sort of omen or portend, although it very well may be. I see that my energy is vast and abundant, it has engulfed me and it has been diligently making me face myself. My desire for physicality and sexual intimacy has been unusually high, and as I have kept it under wraps it still finds its way to revisit. Not even while allowing myself to be in temptation, I am now in a relationship with myself that I see I am seeking. Not for conquest or belief that I am defined by my phallus. Not merely as a form of art, expression, wisdom, healing, and growth. I now see sexual energy as more of a vessel not merely for procreation but a medium to bring therapy, self-cognizance, and clarity. It may seem a bit Erie but somehow it does not feel lustful or more so merciful. A tool not used for destruction but for redemption. I am currently struggling with this notion. I am also currently celibate, yet I find my urges growing very strong and I am without a doubt, properly analyzing the triggers. Maybe feedback or understanding is what I need to search for. I will revisit this here soon! In the meantime, my focus has to remain as it is quite obvious something may be arising here soon!

Dear Diary,

It has been a while since I have come to you. Today I am finding an eternal balance between my beliefs vs. my ego vs. expectations vs. my standards. Somehow, they align ever so often and most of the time cannot seem to agree like when I ask my woman what she wants to eat. I am picking up a few habits but I will not jinx them as for now it is in the slow process of moving along and understanding how to maneuver. I like challenges, I really do Yet somewhere I stopped and I for the life of me have no fucking clue as to why. I was psycho analyzed and it blew my mind yet it was relieving. Plenty of times I am the sounding board for others and while taking in others' trauma I battle with my own. In need of expression, I tend to fall into deep repressive patterns where I self-implode. Nobody knows though it is a tale of pride and self-deprecation which ultimately, I think stands in my way. I hide it well like I am loyal to my own agony. I am more times than not my greatest obstacle and it manifests in my material world. I am seeking a feeling of something just right and I can say up until this point I have not. I have not found a home; I have not found refuge. I have found my vast array of possibilities and it continues to grow daily. So, the uneasiness in myself is the guiding light telling me to continue searching and eventually it will all be revealed. In the meantime, I will enjoy it all.

Dear Diary,

You know I woke up today finding myself in a frenzy. Frantically believing that my self-confidence was merely a mirage. That it was a fabric of lesser quality. The wait is my ideal passion fleeting. Trends find no enrichment in my soul. How unnatural I feel in the presence of the average. Swaying my perception, I battle my thoughts. Then polemic I attack the previous and come to a separate conclusion.

Wow, today I woke up to a lie and I caught it and as I held it then swiftly let it fly free. My self-esteem is not a facade but an earned treasure. I now understand it is self-induced. Extrinsic quality does not quantify it, intrinsic energy drives but somehow just divine spirit defines, fortifies, and sources it.

Breaking is a part of the process, falling is the lesson, failing is the test, and disappointment is the bargain. For glory comes not to those who easily look to obtain it, how could I be so blind I knew of these teachings. I possessed these tools; I believed I had to carry it all that it was mine alone to conquer. Such folly to designate an immeasurable and infinite role to such a limited space.

Today felt like: a weakness leaving my body...

ELEVATION

Dear Diary,

    I have been observing Ramadan to enlighten my spiritual palette and connect with a higher power and source. This will be my second year participating and although I am relatively new, It intrigued me the discipline and overall experience it brings. My mind is a bit sharper due to a change in diet, intermittent fasting, and the motion of purpose set behind the trying month. Tonight, will be the end officially, and I am never truly good with endings. They always seemed to be storybooks or made up. I am struggling with this belief I am carrying and right now my writing is not the avenue to release it. I find trouble in expressing my truest heart desires but in them, I find this utopia with which my life can blossom, bear fruit, and inspire. Yet I am sure of 2 things the world has yet to see me in pure form and fashion. Today I realized that I am something many desires yet in raw form. I am what men yearn to embody and without thoughts, I am physically capable and blessed. Women may say they are against it and not in pursuit of it but many would appreciate being in the presence of it. Today I allowed someone else to show me myself. It showed a side that some would call not correct.

    I would simply like to say FUCK those some, you are just mad you cannot be one.

    Today was TRANSPARENT

Diary,

I get weary, I get tired, I get lonely, I find doubts, I experience heartache, I feel pain, I find obstacles, and I tussle with struggles. As a man, I go through silent bouts of depression, angst, uncertainty, confusion, and lack of discipline.

I then look at those very issues head-on and remind myself that I am strong, I am wise and capable, I am resilient, I am tough, I am savvy, I am blessed.

Some days I yearn for what is not available to me: companionships, luxury, leisure, celebrations, my deep desires, and passions. Intimacy is sometimes above all else.

Then as I climb my mountain, and rest atop its alone eye to eye with the moon. I simply bask in the fact that if I were to stop, I would do myself a disservice.

So, I continue: some days battered, some days refreshed, others stressed, yet every day from here on out.

I will remain Focused!

Dedication and devotion go far for all people, it makes sense for men. It is the defining characteristic of creating an experience from knowledge, wealth from riches, and blessings from turbulence. Without the dedication and focus you cannot quite accomplish anything. If God took days to create the heavens and earth as we know it, as a man merely mortal— dedication is arguably the best and most reasonable way to create my own paradise.

Dear Diary,
I find myself needing solace and solitude.
Contradicting it may sound but I do not see it as such.
Yet sometimes it is how I find comfort in my own presence and loneliness among others.

I understand that they will never understand me (word to Rick Ross)

Peace comes at times of discouragement and disappointing outcomes, merely conditioned by the expectation and experience of that.

I am wiping the slate clean through mental and heart methods. Nobody should expect dissatisfaction, or loss, and not be balanced in some form of joy or success.

So,

I am slowly finding salvation in the community. I have attended group meditation and bible study over the past almost 2 years.

Though once a week and sometimes not even that it has mended my doubts about the outside world.

Not by much but substantially compared to where I once stood with society.

Maybe my awareness is better, my naïveté has worn off, or I am losing the child-like innocent acceptance I once held sometimes foolishly.

These are becoming therapy sessions, writing like that, and reflecting helps me unravel so much.

As you can see, I thoroughly enjoy ME which has never really been a problem, it is just these days it is far more productive, therapeutic, and revealing.

It felt like kicking a bad habit...

I have had years of surety to a fault in myself, bad habits that at a previous stage of myself were sufficient. My diet is the one in my youth that would only be described as glutton bordering not quite discerning. As I found myself in new instances and ways that I am unfamiliar with naturally my habits kicked in, in one space those habits kept me alive. This new space holds me hostage. Habitual and unconscious acknowledgment is being sure that along the way you will be wrong and need to adjust, that your vices will surface. Catching them before detriment is guaranteed while accepting along the way people, places, and even self-imposed confinement are your decisions that need to be modified & released. The fact is our habit is as much a part of us as men, praise is equal to critique. Yet, along the way the question is: am I holding myself back with habits that no longer propel me forward?

Dear Diary,

Tonight, I find myself at one of my favorite places. The playground is well after hours, it is long gone with any sounds of tag or swings. Just crickets, streetlights, and empty slides. I am in the process of unfolding and releasing the pressure of trying. Resistance has been a huge part of me and now letting go, is all I intend to do. I knew I struggled with control, merely because as a child I felt out of control but obligated to take on responsibility. It is more to problems I did not create. (Let us Revisit this later)

I spent my life making my own messes and then attempting to help clean others up as a distraction. Leaving a blazing trail of destruction in the wake of my own actions and path. The silver lining is how that path will possibly someday be mapped.

Wow, 28, and my life was not painted on the canvas like I envisioned. Pictures are worth a thousand words yet you cannot see all the ones that lie behind the lens. Filter, Angles, and Post have trapped many in time while I seek to step out of the screen and come to life. No doll, yet I was once told I am the Black Ken and can do all things. How true that is I am not quite sure. Yet how confident I am and fearless I have become tells that it very well may be valid.

So, what I have done is draw the line...

Playing only at my leisure, outworking others, then pursuing things I can only imagine. No vision to grand and no obstacle to stifling.

So, I have held my own...

Letting the unwanted feel my absence, while the needy appreciate my presence. This is a boundary and one that makes me not in the slightest feel any form of remorse. No sight of a fuck and no desire to appease anyone not even those I value most.

So, I had a few great and bad examples rolled into one and I assume that is what adulthood and parenthood present to your children. Yet I took it as a personal mission. That mess I used to clean up was my parents to fix which to this day they've yet to maturely amend. But 28 years and I can care not an ounce if they do at this point. I cannot carry that weight. It is not even that heavy but not beneficial either.

I trailed a few weak mentors and their words although inspiring mostly smoke and mirrors. I resented them at one point but I forgave them to move forward. They are associates that taught me life's secrets in secret.

I loved a few harlots but I cannot say I had not tried to be the Don to keep them in the nearest proximity. I stepped away and realized it was cute at best and entertainment mostly. The appeal no longer lingers. I fell for a few traps and it is OK because warriors never go out without first being completely destroyed.

Until my soul leaves this plane, my voice will ring, my presence will be felt, and my LEGACY will be ETERNAL. I did not come here to be meek so I FOCUS.

My messes tidied, my goals merely just a new day, and my BEST DAY coming as my NEXT DAY.

Then I just remember that the world is all A PLAYGROUND...

Remember the question, what do you want to be when you grow up. Why don't we ever ask, who will you become as you grow up? Questioning a stationary position that is in proportion to your entire existence is a minority, versus what your maturation means for you. A kid grows to be a Goat, an ewe a Ram, a caterpillar a butterfly, so as humans we should transform by keeping our youthful self as understanding from whence we once came from. Seeing who I was as a child leaves me with clarity of who I have been –yet what is better is who I am becoming. Self-esteem teaches us to love ourselves sincerely and yet men are taught to love themselves conditionally. If I can transform into a version of myself, I can work towards and become willing to accept it in the absence of who I once was, then wouldn't who I become make more sense than what I want to be...?

Dear Diary,

As biblically stated, God is said to come to you in Dreams.

Last night I was given that call which has been a consistent visit here recently.

This was no calm visit as rage was found in this dream. Not in regards to me but through me.

Showing me things my eyes before were too naive to capture. My heart erupted, my mind scrambled, and all resolve was in the form of uncontrolled fury.

I have not felt like this in years. As a youth, I struggled with strong episodes of blackout-type anger. I would cradle my voice and quiet my thoughts to make others comfortable.

After being told my words were too much, too brash, or wrong to say. I began to internalize my own voice which as a child began to sit and fester until it ticked to the explosion.

God showed me things I had not fathomed, yet spoke to me through truth, and through that found me in a place where I needed to be.

I unsheathe my sword of rage and unleashed it on a deserving suitor. I accept that to move forward I needed the vision, the release, and the insight.

God is said to come to you in dreams.

This morning God showered me with rightful and needed expulsion and I do feel it is very intuitive to my life moving forward.

Today felt like clearing a new path to success!

Manhood, although according to propaganda and misinformation is defined in a space of materialism. Definitive identifiers that make a man in line with qualities of importance, power, and manliness. These descriptors are merely an advertisement, a function to define and box masculinity. It is spiritual as is the feminine but more in a concrete or actionable way. Masculinity is the heart pulsing and the aura & vibration it gives.

Masculinity at its peak is pure spiritual strength, a leading function to move and progress. While clearing a path is a function of a healthy masculine, the messiness and disorganized masculine is a masculine with no routine and unhealthy clogging his own path. When God speaks to me and I listen intently & surrender to strive ahead to my manhood it may come with the materialism of titles, monetary gains, and adult toys. Yet the truth is honestly, manhood is far more than marketable definitions but more so intrinsic qualities and character that align with a man's soul. Those are powerful, important, and manly!

Diary,

Moment of truth— I struggle with intimacy, more so in the form of both Platonic and intimate relationships. I am used to people leaving, and I am accustomed to change and variation. Stability was not provided to me as a youth. I was moved and tussled with the lack of balance and consistency. Hence my own lack thereof.

Even worse I at one point was addicted if not overly overrun by lustful desire. Logging onto explicit sites to satisfy my craving for some type of connection. Yet it was safe, with no rejection, stability, and lack of life's fears.

I was once accused of sexual assault, what I knew to be a consensual encounter that then was a change of heart and respected by me, which ultimately turned into a nightmare. I knew I could not bear to even go through with an act like such, yet here I was accused of something I in my years never felt was justifiable to any degree. I sat in courtrooms praying that I would not face prison time but worse face the removal from my son, the one person who loved me unconditionally despite my abundance of flaws and imperfections.

That occurrence scarred me beyond recovery. I secluded myself and vowed to almost refrain from sex unless it was explicitly initiated by the woman (whom I had to have some longevity and utmost familiarity with) and even then, I felt no ease. Found myself battling with even approaching women. These years before "Me Too" or countless accusations arose against men for past transgressions or perceived ones.

I battled with the desires and my want to satisfy, protect, and love a woman, apparently, a feat, as I've yet to grasp it properly. A single father of two and have not had a significant other in years. While all past relationships have crumbled and deteriorated.

I sit and revel in the destruction like, " look what you've done."

Wow, my doubts play constant partners with these demonic shameful occurrences.

I have been sexually abstinent for quite some time. More so for various reasons. Days I yearn for a consistent lover and then sporadically I desire spontaneous and wild inhibition.

I have come to terms with my feelings and past. My heart has calmed due to knowing exactly who I am and who I am not. I have also accepted that my libido is no obstacle or hindrance but merely a part of me.

I am still practicing intimacy and building continuity but I am learning from a blank canvas. The only recollection I have of my parents is screaming and yelling matches that ended with no resolution. Two adults with terrible communication have trickled into their offspring so maybe I will start there and hopefully, it will help my intimacy issues.

I know I shared a lot, but I could not continue to judge and jury myself internally, as it has literally worn me down.

Until we meet again, thank you for being an intimate space so that I can share my vulnerability. I appreciate you in ways that only the words on your pages can be expressed.

Again, thank you for following my expression. It was necessary to share this! I pray it was necessary for you to read it.

-DIARY OF A MAN

The goal of this was never to be a space of anything other than the complexity and truth that is manhood [particularly my expression and perception of it], at an intersection of my ethnic roots and my ideology that is not status quo. Social conformity has never aligned with me, an intimate opening to what I needed which was vulnerability. If opening up and sharing my thoughts, emotions, soul, and heart on many levels can be a healthy space in this current world, I pray that healing and abundance covers you. As these are intimate and personal entries to my journal, I knew it necessary to be open and show that as men we battle with our own existence. That our emotions may not fully show but move like others. Men it is ok to be unsure or in need of help or guidance, it is equally alright to find outlets that build you up and do not tear you down. The step towards building your manhood is your own, not your parents, not spouses/significant others, children if you are blessed, or any external factor. It is your design; you are the architect along with God's guidance to be the vessel that provides provision, protection, wisdom, strength, leadership, and humility amongst so many other attributes.

Epilogue

This book was years of experience, life, and more than a handful of moments of reflection. The nature of me sharing not only intimate thoughts and self-induced engagements was a truth that in my experience is a valuable piece. Many boys never cross the threshold into manhood because we are groomed as that's just the way boys are until society teaches us as men –you can't just be whatever you want to be. I find that notion to be absurd, when I chose to actively take full control of my existence and life, it came with sacrifices, hard work, but novel & genuine truth. Showing myself who I really was placed here to be and serving the purpose God has of me is far more important than living meek. These words are all of my own thoughts, actions, and admission that young boys & men have things we stow away. Those very things are heavy and light but sometimes accumulate and need a place to be set down appropriately. This book, this expression is that very place for myself. Many of these thoughts sat with me for years before I felt compelled to share them, others never saw the day of light until now. My genuine desire and hope is to tell young men of all walks, your manhood is yours to define and live and as you fall remain steadfast and keep getting up until you become unshakeable. My father was absent for most of my life but the men God placed around me allowed me to pick parts that would help me mold myself into the man I saw myself as. Even with having parts, knowing the tools and their use, along with having a clear plan and vision are still very integral parts of me. The goal was to quiet the hurt little boy's fears, the timid childs apprehensions, and the naive young man's folly. This Diary is but just a small fraction of the amount of work that has gone into becoming my best and truest form! Along with each entry and excerpt comes a million more ideas, moments, and even shortcomings that made this very book come to life. If change can start from the inside while also becoming the very way in which you live then you too can embrace the journey and freedom as well as the responsibility and success of MANHOOD.

ABOUT THE AUTHOR

Johnny Hall is the product of a variety of experiences and moments in a young and early stage of his curated life. As he has grown, words, teaching, and learning have become an integral part of him, the focus to always find truth even at his own expense. While his life is not a source of societal normalcy, his life is a variance of variety & journey. Being exposed to vastness has helped pour into him and has created every fiber of who he has become and yet to build upon. A man still building upon his own legacy. This is Johnny Hall's first published book with intent to build upon his desire to both help and express through his own wisdom, life experiences, and thoughts along the way. As a young man, father, son and many other facets his goal is to embody himself and what that masculine energy exudes and utilize his gifts as connection to the world.

www.ingramcontent.com/pod-product-compliance
Ingram Content Group UK Ltd.
Pitfield, Milton Keynes, MK11 3LW, UK
UKHW042004230426
12048UKWH00009B/531